VERY
Unusual
PETS

by Howard Gutner

Modern Curriculum Press
Parsippany, New Jersey

Credits

Photos: All photos ©Pearson Learning unless otherwise noted.
Front cover: Dan McCoy/Rainbow. Title page: Michael Habicht/Animals Animals. 5:
©Renee Lynn/Photo Researchers, Inc. 6: Clifford Keeney/New England Stock. 7:
Nancy Shepherd/Pig O' My Heart Potbellies. 8: Eastcott/Momatiuk/Animals Animals.
9: D. Fisher Foto, courtesy of Mary Kaye Ashley/American Domestic Skunk
Association. 10: Christian Mundt/Unicorn Stock. 11, 12: Mary Kaye Ashley/American
Domestic Skunk Association. 13: David Liebman. 14: Nancy Shepherd/Pig O' My Heart
Potbellies. 15: Chris Boylan/Unicorn Stock. 16: ©Tim Davis/Photo Researchers, Inc.
17: Norvia Behling/Behling & Johnson Photography. 18: Scott Trees/Paintbrush
Miniature Horses. 19: ©Francois Gohier/Photo Researchers, Inc. 20: Dan
McCoy/Rainbow. 22: Joan McGee. 23: Priscilla Valentine/Valentines Performing
Pigs.Computer

Cover and book design by Lisa Ann Arcuri

Modern Curriculum Press
An imprint of Pearson Learning
299 Jefferson Road, P.O. Box 480
Parsippany, NJ 07054–0480

www.pearsonlearning.com

1-800-321-3106

ISBN: 0–7652–1361-3

3 4 5 6 7 8 9 10 UP 08 07 06 05 04 03 02 01 00

Contents

To all those who make room in their
hearts and homes for a pet

CHAPTER 1

You Have a What?

You may know a lot of people who have a dog or a cat. You might have a friend who has a bird or a fish. These are pets that many people have.

A boy plays with his cat.

A girl holds her pet snake.

An unusual pet is an animal that most people would not think of as a pet. Some people keep snakes as pets. Other people keep skunks or pigs. Many people like to keep big green lizards called green iguanas.

Where do people find pets like skunks and pigs? You can't find them at most pet stores. Many people buy these pets from people who already own them. When the pets have babies, their owners may sell the babies. The owners may also give them away to good homes.

Joel with Munchkin and her litter of piglets

Sometimes people find animals in the woods. They take them home and turn them into pets. This is not a good idea. Wild animals should not be kept as pets. They are not used to people. It would be better for the animals if they were left alone.

A little boy meets a slider turtle.

Pet Fact More people own cats than any other kind of pet.

CHAPTER 2

A Skunk in the House

The people who have skunks for pets would not give them away. They don't want a dog or cat. Just ask Mary Kaye Ashley.

Ashley has had pet skunks for nearly 20 years. She helps people learn how to take care of pet skunks.

Mary Kaye Ashley with her skunk, Max

Many people think that skunks smell bad. That's not true. Skunks have glands in their bodies that make a liquid. It is the liquid that smells bad.

A skunk may think another animal is going to hurt or chase it. That is when the skunk sprays the liquid. The other animal usually runs away fast!

A wolf is sprayed by a skunk.

Skunk inside a suitcase

Before people buy a skunk as a pet, they have the glands taken out. Still, it's not always easy living with a skunk. Skunks are very curious animals. They will open drawers. They will look in backpacks. They might even crawl into a washing machine or a suitcase!

Skunk crawling out of a sneaker

Skunks also like to hide things! They will take shirts. They will steal socks left on the floor. They might even take a blanket off a bed and drag it across a room. Sometimes they hide little things in shoes.

What do people feed their pet skunks? Skunks like fruit such as oranges and vegetables such as lettuce. They also like chicken, fish, yogurt, and rice. We can all learn about eating good food from what a skunk has for dinner.

Pet Fact Skunks can come in many colors! They are not always black and white. Some are all white. Some are very light purple.

A white skunk

CHAPTER 3

Pets From the Farm

Some people turn farm animals into pets. A sheep, a goat, or a chicken can be a family pet.

Some people have unusual farm animals as pets. They may have tiny horses no bigger than some dogs. They may keep pot-bellied pigs, too.

Samantha makes friends with Twinkie.

Pot-bellied pigs grow to about three feet long. They weigh about 100 pounds. This is much smaller than other pigs.

Pot-bellied pigs come from a country called Vietnam. They were brought to the United States in the 1980s.

A boy feeds his pot-bellied pig.

At first you could only see pot-bellied pigs in zoos. Then some people found out that these pigs make good pets.

What's so great about pot-bellied pigs? They are very clean. They are also very friendly. They do not bark or chew up shoes like some dogs. Because they are very smart, pot-bellied pigs are very easy to train. They like to learn tricks!

A pot-bellied pig picks up a telephone.

Children pet a mini-horse.

Other unusual pets from the farm are little horses. Miniature horses are about two feet tall. That is the size of many large dogs! Many people call these small horses minis.

Mini-horses are different from dogs. You can't keep little horses in your house. You would need a barn and a large yard!

Mini-horses are just like big horses. They come in the same colors as bigger horses. They eat hay. They make sounds like big horses. They can be trained, too, but they are too small to ride.

A mini-horse pulls a cart.

 Pet Fact Minis are small but strong. They can easily pull people in a wagon.

CHAPTER 4

A Dinosaur of Your Own!

What do you think it would be like to have a dinosaur as a pet? Dinosaurs lived on Earth a long, long time ago. Now they are all gone. However, some people have pets that look like dinosaurs. These pets are iguanas.

A wild iguana

A boy feeds his pet iguana.

Green iguanas are lizards that some people keep as pets. A few iguanas grow to be five or even six feet long. Iguanas that long might look like dinosaurs.

You might wonder what iguanas eat. Iguanas are plant eaters. They like to eat oranges and carrots. They also like strawberries and green beans.

An iguana's cage should be the right size. It should be twice as big as the animal. If you have a large iguana, you will need a big cage! Some people who have iguanas give them a room of their own in the house.

An iguana in a glass case

An iguana also needs a bowl of clean water in its cage. The iguana will not drink very often, but without water it will die. If the water bowl is big enough, the iguana may take a bath. Some people let their iguanas swim in their swimming pools.

An iguana sits by a pool.

Would you like to share your room with an iguana? Maybe you would rather have a skunk or a pig for a pet. As you now know, there are all kinds of unusual pets!

A pig jumps through a hoop.

Pet Fact
A pet iguana will take a dip in the bathtub if there is no swimming pool.

Glossary

chase [chays] run after a person or animal

curious [CYOOR ee us] wanting to find out about something

gland [gland] part of the body that changes things from the blood for the body to use or give off

lettuce [LEH tus] garden plant with large green leaves

liquid [LIH kwud] something that flows like water

miniature [MIH nee uh chur] very small

unusual [un YOO zhuh wul] strange or different

yogurt [YOH gurt] thick liquid food made from milk